THE FORGOTTEN ART OF BUILDING A GOOD FIREPLACE

FRONTISPIECE

THE FIREPLACE, ILLUSTRATED ON THE VERSO OF THIS PAGE, IS IN THE LIBRARY OF MY HOUSE IN WESTON, VERMONT. THE HEARTH AND CURVED BACK OF THE FIREPLACE ARE LAID IN BRICK: THE COVINGS AND FIREBACK ARE 4-INCH-THICK SLABS OF SOAPSTONE, QUARRIED IN VERMONT, WHICH SERVES TO HOLD THE HEAT AFTER THE FIRE HAS GONE OUT.

OBSERVATIONS ON
The Forgotten Art
OF BUILDING A GOOD FIREPLACE

The Story of *Sir Benjamin Thompson*, COUNT RUMFORD,
an American Genius, & his *Principles* of
Fireplace Design which have *Remained*
Unchanged for 174 *Years*

By VREST ORTON, *Esq.re*
Former Chairman VERMONT HISTORIC SITES COMMISSION
& President AMERICAN ASSOCIATION OF
HISTORIC SITES OFFICIALS

PUBLISHED MCMLXXIV BY

YANKEE BOOKS

DUBLIN   NEW HAMPSHIRE

16th Printing, 1986

SECOND EDITION

Copyright 1974, by Vrest Orton

First Edition 1969

DEDICATION

To my wife, Ellen, who has endured my observations

FOREWORD

PART I

A Biographical Account of Sir Benjamin Thompson,
Count Rumford

PART II

The Riddle of the Modern Fireplace
and Its Shortcomings

PART III

Benjamin Franklin's Observations on Fireplaces

PART IV

Count Rumford's Principles
of Fireplace Design

Drawings & Diagrams by Austin Stevens

Foreword

YEARS AGO we hired a mason and his helper to do some plastering in our house, built in 1828. In one room is a fireplace with a front opening 42 inches tall and a depth of only 19 inches. I overheard the mason exclaim to his helper, "Look at that funny fireplace! With *that* opening it won't draw!"

We had been burning wood in this fireplace for some years and enjoying the flames as they leapt up fully twenty-four inches high without the slightest whiff of smoke: the fireplace always "drew" like a house-a-fire and still does. (*See Frontispiece*).

My curiosity was aroused. Since evidence demonstrated that the fireplace was not wrong, the masons must be.

This little episode was the beginning of this book.

From that day, I consulted masons, builders, architects and contractors, and they all calculated that a fireplace 42 inches tall and 19 inches deep was a funny fireplace. The proper fireplace, in their view, should be no taller than its depth: in short, if you have one 19 inches deep, you must have one no more than 19 inches tall! Why? Because they knew taller fireplaces would smoke, and never "draw."

It was then that I began to wonder. My fireplaces were two to three times taller than the depth and they all worked beautifully. Could it be that the old-time masons who made the brick and laid them up into my house and fireplaces, 140 years ago, were completely wrong? Or were contemporary masons, architects and builders the wrong ones?

I thought that I had better find out. It did not take long. A brief scanning of cards in the New York Public Library under *Fireplaces* soon led me to a name then unknown to me:— Sir Benjamin Thompson, Count Rumford. Research at the American Antiquarian Society and at the Public Library, both in Worcester, Massachusetts, led me quickly to Count Rumford's then unknown work on fireplaces,[1] and Benjamin Franklin's also forgotten speculations on the same.[2]

---

[1]*Chimney Fireplaces with Proposals for Improving Them to Save Fuel, to Render Dwelling Houses More Comfortable and Salubrious, and Effectually to Prevent Chimneys from Smoking.*

[2]*A Letter from Dr. B. Franklin to Dr. Ingen-hausz, Physician to the Emperor, at Vienna. In TRANSACTIONS of the American Philosophical Society Held at Philadelphia for Promoting Useful Knowledge. Philadelphia, MDCCLXXXVI.*

Like any amateur historian I knew something about Franklin. But now to discover another genius of similar, if not equal, stature, was a thrilling experience not unlike that of Cortez in Keat's immortal words:—

Then I felt like some watcher of the skies
When a new planet swims into his ken;

This is why, in this small book, I have dwelt not alone on Rumford's ways of building a fireplace, but considerably on Count Rumford, the man.

It will be obvious to the reader that my admonitions, asides and philippics interlarded with those of Rumford and Franklin are, as were theirs (if I may be presumptuous), in the same conservative tradition. This, I submit, in dealing with a subject as traditional as fireplaces and 18th century geniuses, is as it should be.

If the reader will accept my definition of *Conservative*, he may more readily accept the reason. A conservative is a person whose knowledge of history compels him to an admiration of, and a respect for, the wisdom of the ages and the great men responsible for such. And (here is the point) he wishes to conserve it!

Dr. Russell Kirk, whose great books on the conservative tradition are daily winning more Americans to a new respect for the wisdom of the past, always quotes, to emphasize this point, Edmund Burke, who said that we are but pygmies standing on the shoulders of giants!

If we did not thus stand, how could we see the distant horizon!

{13}

Benjamin Franklin, no one denies, was one of these giants. Many may, I hope, see that Franklin's contemporary Sir Benjamin Thompson, Count Rumford, stands near him in that noble and permanent niche in history.

Since this book treats of giants and the principles they formulated as to the science of heat and the construction of fireplaces, it would be fruitless to dwell on the little details that all good masons once well knew and (so I hope) still practice. You won't find here instructions to masons on how to mix mortar, how to lay brick, or how to build a chimney around a ceramic flue. But you may find a little evidence that you can use as ammunition to make them practice well their ancient craft.

VREST ORTON

Weston, Vermont
May 1969.

{*14*}

PART I

A Biographical Account
of Sir Benjamin Thompson
Count Rumford

It was a most remarkable man who, in writing the first and still (after 174 years) the best book on fireplace design, could have included such a practical subject in a volume with the formidable title of "ESSAYS: POLITICAL, ECONOMICAL AND PHILOSOPHICAL".[1]

---

[1]*This dual nature of philosophy and science always co-existent with the practical and useful is the key to Sir Benjamin Thompson's life. Professor Sanborn C. Brown, the leading American authority on Count Rumford and his work, sums up this character by saying, "Here was a man of real scientific imagination and persistence, who developed a number of important theories from careful observations, a physicist who championed our modern research method of studying fundamentals before trying to make practical applications."*

{*15*}

His contribution to the art of the fireplace made him outstanding enough; his life made him unique. A Massachusetts farmer's son, born at Woburn in 1753, he was at 20 a Major in the New Hampshire militia and by the time his treatise on fireplaces was published in London in 1795 he could legitimately place on the title page his noble title *Count of Rumford.* He had been created Count of the Holy Roman Empire in 1792, taking his style from Rumford, his wife's birthplace . . . now, of course, Concord, the capitol city of New Hampshire.

He was knighted by King George III of England in 1784; decorated by the King of Poland in 1786. He designed the famous and unique English Garden in Munich, Germany, and it was the Elector (reigning monarch) of Bavaria, Karl Theodor, who made him a Count and, in 1798, appointed him Minister Plenipotentiary to the Court of St. James's and posted him to London as Bavarian diplomatic representative when Rumford already held a commission of Colonel in the British Army.

No one denies the wide range of his talent or that he led one of the most remarkable lives of any man of his time. This fact was succinctly expressed on the title page of his book where, after his name, appear the following honors:—"*Knight of the Order of the White Eagle, and of St. Stanislaus; Chamberlain, Privy Counsellor of State, Lieutenant-General in the Service of his Most Serene Highness, the Elector Palantine, Reigning Duke of Bavaria; Colonel of his Regiment of Artillary;*

{16}

*Commander in Chief of the General Staff of His Army;
F. R. S. Acad.; R. Hiber.; Berol.; Elec.; Bicoi.; Palat. et
Amer. Soc. . .".*

He was an American and his name was Benjamin
Thompson. Apprenticed in 1766 to a country store
keeper in Salem, Massachusetts, he worked as a clerk
and later as an apprentice to a well-known Woburn
physician, Dr. Hay, but constantly studied on his own
and undertook a series of remarkable and successful
scientific experiments in his spare time. Even at four-
teen, he was sufficiently advanced in algebra, geometry,
astronomy and higher mathematics to calculate a solar
eclipse within four seconds of absolute accuracy.

At nineteen, he says, "I married, or rather I *was*
married." This subtle distinction explains how Benjamin
Thompson came under the benevolent aegis of John
Wentworth, Royal Governor of New Hampshire,
through his wife's connections. She was the widow of
Colonel Benjamin Rolfe and her father was one of the
first settlers of Rumford, New Hampshire. She had
inherited a respectable amount of property and was
several years Thompson's senior.

In spite of these circumstances, fortuitous as they
were, or calculated as they appear to be, I believe it was
due to Thompson's precocity and personality that he
made a hit with Governor Wentworth, rather than to
his wife's money. At any rate, young Benjamin Thompson's own sense of loyalty to King George III, enhanced
by his association with British General Gage, command-
ing the King's troops in Boston, as well as with the

King's Royal Governor of the province of New Hampshire, placed him in disrepute with the radicals of Boston, then led by the fervent and irresponsible Samuel Adams. [2] General Thomas Gage, in 1776, after the evacuation of Boston by the royal troops, was wise enough to select Thompson as a courier to carry official dispatches to Lord Germain in England.

Certainly Lord George Germain, Secretary of State for the Colonies, could have been influenced only by the genius and ability of this young man who, then 23 years old, was appointed private secretary to the British Minister. Four years later Thompson was advanced to the position of Under Secretary of State for the Colonies. This was not an inconsiderable position under the British Crown. In 1779, he was elected fellow of the prestigious Royal Society and when the American War for Independence ended in 1783, Benjamin Thompson held a royal commission of Lieut. Colonel in a British Regiment, later to be promoted full Colonel.

Following his successes in England, Thompson's fortunes broadened to the European scene through an introduction to the Elector who reigned as the Monarch of the Kingdom of Bavaria. Here Benjamin Thompson spent probably the most famous, productive and certainly interesting decade of his life. Made upon arrival

---

[2]*Because Benjamin Thompson took no pains to hide his feelings that he was loyal to the forces of law and order, as represented by King George III, he was soon denounced as a traitor, hauled before a Committee of Safety and nearly tarred and feathered by the mob in Concord, New Hampshire, before he escaped into Boston.*

aide-de-camp to the Elector, he served in various and distinguished portfolios of rank and office such as Colonel, later General of the Bavarian Army, Minister of War, Grand Chamberlain of the Court, Minister of Police and was soon the highest ranking person at the Court, next to the Monarch himself.

The many honours and duties, however, were not too onerous to this versatile and ambitious young American to prevent him from devoting time and thought to science and to what today we would call the "War on Poverty". But with a more practical twist than practiced in our 20th century.

Minister Thompson found, as anyone could not help finding in the late 18th century, and assuredly as one finds today, that mendicity was a most popular career. In Bavaria this well-organized and powerful multitude of beggars and hoodlums had become a conspicuous burden on and even a danger to the state. Thompson did not, as 20th century liberals have done, award free sloth with free income. Instead he rounded up in Munich, in one day alone, 2600 of these beggars, incarcerated them in a place he had prepared for their efforts and then fed them. But only when they worked.

And work they did to such an extent that by making clothing for the army, they soon earned a surplus to enhance the coffers of the State. The words Thompson used to describe this experiment in curing the indigent are as admirable as they are unique. He said, "To make vicious and abandoned people happy, it has generally been supposed necessary first to make them virtuous.

But why not reverse the order? Why not make them first happy, and then virtuous?"

Explaining the condition in which he found this mob, Thompson declared that "they were so attached to their indolent and dissolute way of living as to prefer it to all other situations. They were not only unacquainted with all kinds of work but had the most insuperable aversion to honest labor, and had been so long familiarized with every crime that they had become perfectly calloused to all sense of shame and remorse . . ."

Benjamin Thompson's wisdom comes across the centuries to us today in many ways. But no more profitable and useful general advice did this genius bequeath to our age than this simple fact:— *to make people happy teach them to work and, when they work, they will no longer be dependent on the State!*

In 1799 Thompson, now Count Rumford, founded, with Sir Joseph Banks, the Royal Institution of Great Britain[3] for scientific research and study and selected as lecturer there Sir Humphry Davy whose niche in the history of science is also secure.

Amongst Rumford's other notable and surely numerous distinctions, we must add that he established the Rumford Medal of the distinguished American Academy of Arts and Sciences and the Rumford Chair of Natural Philosophy at Harvard University.

------

[3] *This famous British institution is best described by Prof. Sanborn C. Brown who says that it turned out to be "the first museum of science for the instruction of the general public on the improvement of practical devices in the scientific world."*

A TYPICAL 18TH CENTURY MAN

Being a typical 18th century man (and such men were versatile indeed) these honors were only formal measures of Rumford's genius.

He was, next to Franklin, the most original spirit of his era. He was interested in everything that was not settled and he probed the unknown in all directions.

He turned his inquiring mind to such subjects as how to make soldiers fight better by feeding them better. He completely reorganized the Bavarian Army. He looked into the abuses of usury and improving the breed of horses and cattle. He invented a system of naval signalling, undertook a study of the tensile strength of silk and the warming qualities of wool cloth, and made great advances in military logistics. His discovery of convection currents, the photometer, the method of boring cannon, the nutritious feeding of troops, the calorimeter to measure the heat combustion in wood, coal and other fuels, a modern method of the organization of hospitals and almshouses, the use of portable cooking utensils, the invention of the first drip coffee pot and of a system for heating houses by steam were major innovations, any one of which would have entitled him to a permanent niche in history.

He also improved the lot of working people by instructing them in domestic economy. He saved Munich by sheer diplomacy from an invasion by the armies of Austria and France. He made major advances in the lighting of houses, the manufacture of gunpowder and in the art and science of cooking and baking . . . and not the least, of course, in building and correcting fireplaces so they would never smoke.

In fact, he made original and what were then daring contributions to the science of heat, being the first to discover that heat was not, as then thought, a concrete substance but was produced by the motion of particles.

From these experiments he was the first to understand and use the term *radiant* heat.

He was a military genius of the first degree and contributed in a large way to tactics and strategy in this field. Yet he could, in spite of his accomplishments and his world renown, modestly state that "most of the improvements in the affairs of men, have been made under the pressure of necessity," which is surely a statement of which Benjamin Franklin would have been proud.

Yet today this man Benjamin Thompson, Count Rumford, is in our country literally unknown.

I submit that he is the most neglected American of genuine stature in history.

The neglect comes from the fact that historians were first patriots and then historians. Rumford fled Boston because he felt himself to be, as many did, a loyal subject of King George III. He was thus dubbed a Tory . . . despised by the radicals then, as he would be today, because he was a conservative. One-sided writers simply left him out of history.

In 1964 there was published a full length biography of Rumford, entitled KNIGHT OF THE WHITE EAGLE

SIR BENJAMIN THOMPSON, COUNT RUMFORD, OF WO-
BURN, MASS., by Wilfred James Sparrow, head of the
Department of Education, at the University of Birming-
ham, England. Since 1876 when the American Academy
of Arts and Sciences published the life of Rumford,
written by *Reverend* G. E. ELLIS, there have been
several books on Rumford most of them by Dr. Sanborn
C. Brown. [4]

I certainly disagree with Sparrow's curious statement
that "he (Rumford) was in no field a genius for posterity
to acclaim, but when he died he had become an international figure almost as famous as Benjamin Franklin." I can not, however, disagree with Professor Sparrow's remarkable ability to create a perfect non
sequitur.

The reason for this attitude of a faculty liberal is that
the liberal revisionists of history have written Count
Rumford out of American and British history. The
word *Tory*, to today's liberals, is anathema. This re-
minds me of a good definition given years ago by Ken-
neth Roberts, who has one of his characters in OLIVER
WISWELL say: "Tory! What in God's name does it
mean, anyway!— Any man who runs contrary to the
wishes of the mob is called a Tory! Anybody who wants
to see this country at peace again instead of divided and

----

[4]*Dr. Brown, distinguished physicist and scholar and now Associ-
ate Dean of the Graduate School at Massachusetts Institute of Tech-
nology, is editor of the six volume edition of Count Rumford's works,
now being published by the Harvard University Press. Two volumes
have been issued. The others will follow over the years; the last will
be Dr. Brown's definitive biography of Rumford.*

wrecked by civil war is called a Tory! Every man of property who doesn't talk publicly like a hypocrite and an idiot is called a Tory." Although this definition applied to the 18th century, Rumford's time, its validity today is astonishing.

However, Rumford was not the only 18th century man of genius who fled these shores but whose work stands. One of our country's greatest portrait painters, who left us such a rich heritage of the likenesses of Colonial personages, was John Singleton Copley. He too was loyal to his King but was dubbed a *Tory* and obliged to leave the Colonies. No one, so far as I know, has proved that Mr. Copley's adherence to his King lessened the importance of his art. Today Copley is indubitably granted the accolade of being, with Stuart and West, the most important American artist of the time.

This fact deepens the mystery of why Benjamin Thompson was scratched from the scrolls of history and has remained almost unknown to this day. One reason, apart from the contrived attempt of the historians, might be that, unlike Benjamin Franklin, he did not publish an autobiography and for a very good reason. Thompson prepared one but in a journey to England, in 1795, his private papers and notes for the story of his life were stolen from his postchaise and never recovered.

PART II

The Riddle of
the Modern Fireplace
and its Shortcomings

Count Rumford deserves better than this fateful and contrived oblivion. Even if he had done no more than publish his classic treatise on fireplaces, he would warrant a large niche in the history of those who have benefited mankind. For this unique contribution not only makes very special sense today but demonstrates, beyond cavil, that nearly everything written on the subject of fireplaces since then makes practically no sense at all.

In these last 174 years, one would think that, with all the impressive scientific and technical brains that the world has produced and the incredible advances made in these fields, some new genius would have improved on the work of a man who lived and died before any of our modern domestic conveniences were invented or even dreamt of.

In point of fact, however, everything I have read, published since 1795 on fireplaces, right down to the latest government bulletins either copied what Rumford said, or, in departing from his principles, did nothing but confuse and gave forth wrong and usually dangerous advice which not only made little sense but actually almost destroyed the value of the fireplace in the home.

This is, indeed, a riddle but there is an answer to it.

An Answer To The Riddle

Fireplaces, like many another important feature of the 18th century way of life had, by the late 19th century, become "old-fashioned". As the stove, and later the furnace with central heating, came into general use, fireplaces not only went out of style but went out of houses:— they were bricked up and, in many cases, ripped out and destroyed. It was not until the start of the 20th century that a few persons of good taste and good sense, as well as of some sentiment, began to decry the wholesale destruction of a feature that had meant so much to our ancestors and to appreciate and understand the charming values of the open fire, values both aesthetic and social . . . and often indeed, philosophical.

Measured in cold science, there was no question about the efficiency of stoves and furnaces to produce many more BTU's of warmth. But these modern contraptions produced no other kind of warmth. They could never give forth the bright, cheery, happy qualities of high sparkling flames leaping up in a well-built fireplace nor exert an almost hypnotic influence which drew the family together in a warm and intimate embrace to become the genuine *foyer* of the home. No central heating plant could, people discovered, exude and instill calmness and introspection or create a romantic aura for the building of dreams as did the delightful open fire that came from the clean combustion of aromatic, pungent wood on the open hearth. Nothing else could banish the distractions and irritations of the day so well at evening tide as a fireplace which brought to the family a warmth of mind, heart and spirit.

No one has invented a scientific unit of measurement to test these happy abstractions. It is well that no one has; something needs to be left to human feeling.

So, by the time these amenities of the old-time fireplace became generally recognized again, and accepted by some, it was almost too late for most people to take advantage of them. Many fireplaces that had once been an integral part of the early American house had vanished.

And what made this fact even more tragic, in their place from about 1900 onwards, masons, contractors, builders, village handymen and even architects began to design and construct "modern" fireplaces to meet the new demand. But these sorry versions of the original were so badly designed that they consistently smoked, failed to heat and often failed to burn anything. And they were usually so deep and squatty that they provided neither the kind of warmth that kept people from being cold, nor the aesthetic, social and sentimental warmth that 20th century folk missed and obviously were seeking.

It is a telling commentary on our current civilization to note that at a time when the so-called "Early American" style is all the rage and is manifest in houses, decor, furniture, suburbia, subdivisions, penthouses and even Madison Avenue advertising offices, today's builders and architects, for the most part, have failed miserably to provide, in a proper fashion, the most important feature of early American life. Perhaps if they had, the family would be as closely knit and as important today as it was then.

It is an especially sad commentary to note that in all these 174 years there was available to any serious student who could use a good library, Count Rumford's cardinal principles of fireplace design:— principles as permanent as Euclid's ELEMENTS OF GEOMETRY, and as workable and unchangeable.

How shocked Count Rumford would be, could he view some of the devices that today pass for "fireplaces". One of these examples is a manufactured sheet steel skeleton about which a fireplace may be thrown together of brick veneer. This thing heats the air in the fireplace and attempts to throw the hot air into the room by side escape ducts. The principle is as wrong as the design. Such a fireplace is not only an aesthetic monstrosity and an insult to a good mason, but actually it violates the very principle that Count Rumford discovered:— *fireplace heat is radiant heat*. Radiant heat is cast in straight rays from the fire out into the room and heats bodies and objects that such rays come in contact with, not the air.

If Count Rumford came back today, I would hope to spare him the shock of witnessing that quality and type of brick work done today by masons or, in fact, the quality of the brick.

In a time (his time) before things were carefully calculated to fall apart but on the contrary were built to last, as they did, hundreds of years, the washed handmade brick were of such fine, hard texture and finish that they stood up for generations. Today what bricks are made of I know not, but I presume of sawdust and air, for they disintegrate in about twenty years, and often in less time than that.

Again, I hesitate to speculate on Rumford's comment could he know that instead of laying about 2000 bricks a day, as was formerly an honest day's work for a mason of pride, the Labor Unions have pulled down the daily stint to less than 300.

And the laying of them! Then a good mason took care never to trowel more than a quarter of an inch of fine lime mortar between bricks: today one can see them slop as much as an inch and a half of coarse cement to make a bond. This is why the early brick work stood

{29}

up and it's also why those old walls exhibit such a lovely texture. It is good that the careful men of those early times are not here today to see the slovenly disintegration of their craft.

There are fortunately some exceptions; my advice to the gentleman who wants good brick work and a good fireplace is to make sure that the mason he hires *is* this exception and is willing to build a fireplace according to Rumford's principles and in the careful workmanship of the early masons.

PART III

Benjamin Franklin's Observations
on Fireplaces

WE HAVE ALLUDED to America's greatest genius, Benjamin Franklin, several times in this account, in order to explain Benjamin Thompson as a person. Now we must mention the good Doctor Franklin again, to sharpen and emphasize Benjamin Thompson's unique accomplishment in the art of building fireplaces that never smoked.

For Benjamin Franklin also knew, as did thousands of good folk of those times, that fireplaces did smoke. He wondered why, and speculated on the causes, coming up, in 1785, with some remarks on this subject.

In 1784, the greatest American of his age, at least in the opinion of Europeans, took ship for his last return to his native land. Franklin's distinguished biographer, Carl Van Doren, says that Franklin came home, "The most famous private citizen in the world." He returned after an illustrious and successful mission as American Ambassador to the King of France without whose aid Washington could not have won the war for independence. The Atlantic passage gave Franklin time for introspection and speculation. He characterizes it admirably when he says that . . . "the garrulity of an old man has got hold of me, and, as I may never have another occasion of writing on this subject, I think I may as well now . . .". And so Franklin penned a long letter to his old friend Dr. Ingen-Hausz[1], Physician to the Emperor in Vienna, on the causes and cures of smoky fireplaces. This treatise, the next year, saw the light of print in TRANSACTIONS OF THE AMERICAN PHILOSOPHICAL SOCIETY.

It deserves study for Franklin's inimitable and warmhearted prose. And for us, concerned with Count Rumford, it deserves attention if only for the fact that Franklin, at just about the time Rumford was formulating his ideas which he expressed in print ten years later, discoursed on nine reasons why contemporary fireplaces smoked, and offered remedies to correct such faults. This letter is rich in Franklin's well-known common sense and ingenious experimental devices and is, even today, a sheer delight to read.

[1]*Ingen-Hausz is spelled in this manner in the 18th century.*

But only two of Franklin's nine reasons were demonstrated valid by Rumford's experiments and reasoning. The other seven were not taken up by Rumford in his 1795 treatise because his principles demonstrated that these seven reasons no longer had validity. Fireplaces built according to Rumford's plans, or corrected to his specifications, did not smoke because Franklin's reasons had been disposed of by Rumford's great work.

I do not say that the amiable Franklin, seated in his comfortable ship's cabin in 1784 and writing out of his head, set forth the wrong reasons for smoky fireplaces. I only say that by the time Rumford's work in England was done, no one had any interest in the reasons why Rumford's discoveries were needed by the men and women of that time whose eyes were inflamed by smoke and whose backs (when seated before the fireplace) were cold.

One does not hesitate, however, to recommend Franklin's lengthy remarks for the felicity in which they were expressed and the wit and humor exhibited by this good and happy man.

Benjamin Franklin was writing at a time when no one knew much about heat, and very little about smoke that gets in one's eyes. He remarks that "many are apt to think that smoke is in its nature and of itself specifically lighter than air and rises in it for the same reason that cork rises in water." He soon disposes of this popular notion by proving that smoke is really heavier than air, and that it won't go up a chimney unless heat carries it up.

So Franklin goes to elaborate lengths to show the one reason fireplaces smoke is from want of air in the room. He takes, therefore, the logical position that fresh air must somehow be introduced into the room and he suggests ingenious ways to accomplish this such as opening doors, taking out a pane of glass in the top of a window, and even cutting an opening under the hearth of the fireplace to admit air that the room needs to make the fireplace work.

This is one of the two observations that Rumford knew were valid though, by a strange fate, I do not find anywhere in Rumford's work the mention of Franklin's name, nor in Franklin's the mention of Rumford's.

Franklin's other observation which Rumford did not deny as one of the major reasons for smoky fireplaces was that "a second cause of the smoking of chimneys is their openings in the room being too large; that is too wide, too high, or both."

Rumford's principles of design disposed of this notion. It is interesting to note, however, that Franklin did not develop the notion beyond his opinion that "something" was wrong with the proportions of the fireplace opening in a room. Rumford not only showed that something was wrong, but demonstrated why and how to correct this common defect.

Franklin, however, did advance one interesting idea which puts a floor under my assertion in the beginning and gives me considerable satisfaction that I did not malign or libel architects. Franklin writes that, "Architects in general have no other ideas of proportion in the

{34}

opening of a chimney than that of symmetry and beauty respecting the dimensions of the room . . .".

About the only remark Franklin made in his famous letter that Rumford did not dwell on later was his idea of the size and height of chimneys. Franklin says that, "the openings of the longest funnels may be larger, and that those of the shorter funnels should be smaller." This enlightened many like myself, who enjoy the good fortune of having a house with fireplaces on the first floor and in the bedrooms of the second floor as well. You'll always find, for Franklin's well-considered reason, smaller fireplaces in the second storey rooms than in the first.

And, at this one point, Franklin, in an uncanny fashion almost predicts Rumford's principles when he says, "I would make the openings in my lower rooms about thirty inches square and eighteen deep, and those in the upper, only eighteen inches square and not quite so deep." This remark almost precisely describes the fireplaces in my house and many other early American houses. It foretells as well Rumford's approximate proportions. But Count Rumford, unlike Franklin, demonstrates the reasons and indeed the practical working of his designs, while Franklin only speculates.

It may be helpful to sum up the difference between Franklin's comments and Rumford's work. *Rumford's contributions lay in his understanding of heat, Franklin's of smoke.*

Franklin knew that many fireplaces smoked and he speculated on the physical remedies such as removing

{35}

birds' nests from chimneys and building the chimneys higher than other chimneys or the roof. Rumford also knew that fireplaces smoked. But he went further and found out that they failed to perform the function for which they had been built, which was properly and efficiently to heat a room. To correct these shortcomings in physical design, Rumford studied the nature of heat.

It is an ineluctable fact that both men were geniuses. Rumford went the whole way.

It must also be remembered (and this is seldom remembered) that during the very same time that Franklin was pondering the reasons why fireplaces smoked, he was also dwelling on a method not of making better fireplaces, but of doing away with them.

It was in this period that Franklin devised the stove. As a matter of fact, his paper on stoves, entitled *Description of a New Stove for Burning of Pitcoal, and Consuming All its Smoke* was published in the TRANSACTIONS OF THE AMERICAN PHILOSOPHICAL SOCIETY HELD AT PHILADELPHIA FOR PROMOTING USEFUL KNOWLEDGE along with his letter to Dr. Ingen-Hausz on fireplaces.

I don't attempt to explain this coincidence any more than I would be foolish enough to attempt an explanation of these two American geniuses.

I merely express thanks.

PART IV

Count Rumford's
Principles of Fireplace Design

Count Rumford's principles and practical applications lie buried, as aforementioned, in a rare tome published in England in 1795 and so scarce today that copies may be found only in special libraries known to bibliophiles.

It is extremely unlikely that anyone will come across this volume. Yet, today, it is all the more necessary that these rules be revived and employed because many persons of good taste and discernment are restoring early American houses or hoping to build authentic replicas of the same. Certainly there is no more charming feature of traditional American houses than the fireplace. It seems ridiculous that architects can duplicate all other features of the 18th century decor and then allow masons to put in 1910 fireplaces!

It's so easy to follow Count Rumford's designs and principles.

What are these principles?

Actually they are very simple. But today, when a writer tries to describe something very simple, he is suspect. Most people in our complex era, apparently believe that only the complex has value, even when they don't understand it. The opposite is true.

It is revealing that Count Rumford himself clearly understood this paradox because in 1795 he writes: "I ought to apologize perhaps for having been so very particular in these descriptions . . . I have frequently had to labour to make myself understood, and I only have to express my wishes that my reader may not have been fatigued."

And then he adds that he is setting forth directions for the proper erection of fireplaces so that "gentlemen may undertake to be their own architects."

Today it seems highly probable that gentlemen may, indeed, have to be their own architects of fireplaces because too few contemporary architects seem to know, or take pains to discover, anything about the subject.[1]

---

[1]*There are, of course, exceptions and one architect in Vermont expresses the same unqualified respect for Rumford as I do.*

Smoke Must Rise up The Chimney

Rumford states that, "Since it would be a miracle if smoke should not rise in a chimney (as water runs down hill), we only have to find out and remove these hindrances which prevent smoke from following its natural tendency to rise."

There was nothing like the 18th century logical mind to get at once to the heart of the matter.

One of the major hindrances in the 18th century English fireplaces was the oversized throat, the opening back of the lintel—in short, the space where the fireplace ends and the chimney starts. During his short sojourn in England, Rumford and his masons corrected over 500 fireplaces. In one year his workmen altered over 250 fireplaces in London and soon it became a matter of pride to have a fireplace in one's residence that the famous Count Rumford had supervised.[2]

In practically every case the throat was too big and for a very good reason: there had to be enough space for the chimney sweep to climb from the room up the chimney to clean it out! But as Rumford with his scientific mind reasoned, if you arrange for perfect combustion, the chimney should not get clogged with unburned tars, soots, creosotes, and other foreign matter, and, therefore, you won't need to send little boys up precarious chimneys to swab them out.

---

[2]*If your fireplace does not conform to Rumford's principles set forth here, you may correct it by the use of brick and mortar just the way Rumford and his masons did back in the 18th century.*

Count Rumford was wise enough to know that nothing under the direction of human beings is perfect, including combustion. He knew that people accept changes slowly and that doubtless many would still want to send chimney sweeps up the chimney. So he suggested that they could still do it, if stone blocks in the throat were so arranged that they might be removed to create an opening wide enough for small boys!

GENERAL RULES FOR PERFECT COMBUSTION

In general, Rumford's rules for building new fireplaces and altering old ones were based on practical application of scientific principles. He undertook no step that he had not demonstrated by previous experiment to be scientifically sound and workable.

His basic discovery that heat from a fireplace was radiant heat and proceeded into the room in straight rays, was a foundation for his methods of construction, both as to materials and shape. For example his discovery that good radiating materials were poor reflecting materials caused him to recommend the use of stone or brick back walls instead of iron then generally in use. If heat was to be cast out into the room, which after all was then the purpose of a fireplace, it must be reflected away from the back wall. And further, it must be aided by bevelled sides (called covings) and a slanted back above the vertical fireback, and by the use of smooth materials at back and sides, instead of rough materials.

{40}

Thus it became a simple matter to instruct his masons in the correction of fireplaces in England which, from time immemorial, especially in the castles and halls of stately houses, were massive square boxes, calculated best to roast an ox and freeze an audience. Armed with his geometric principles of design, as to bevelled sides and backs, and of course the size of the throat, it was a simple matter to cause a mason to change the square covings to angled ones, and to build out from the back of the old fireplace, with brick and mortar, the proper shape and depth of the new fireplace.

From these general observations, let me now set down some of Rumford's specific rules.

First rule: Construct the fireplace and the chimney space above it so that a plumb-line dropped from the middle of the throat, both front and back and equal distance from both sides, will fall precisely in the middle of the hearth or floor of the fireplace *(see Diagrams A and B)*. This means, in *Diagram A* half way between *M* and *K* and in *Diagram B* half way between *A* and *B*. Then the smoke, vapour, and unwanted things will go up the chimney and out!

Second rule: Arrange the inside space so that there will be a constant circulation of air when the fire is burning. The warm air goes up the inside front wall of the chimney, and the cold air, from outdoors, comes down the inside back wall of the chimney *(Diagram A)*.

This arrangement, however, is not as simple as it sounds. It is obvious that when the cold air from out-

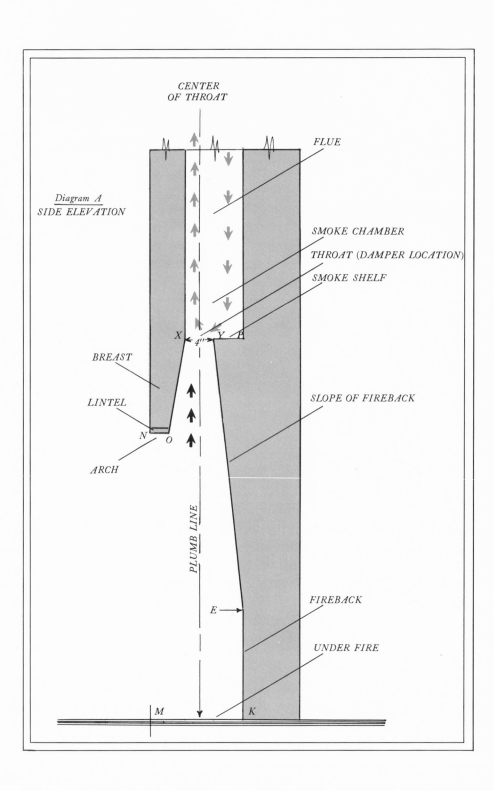

CENTER
OF THROAT

FLUE

Diagram A
SIDE ELEVATION

SMOKE CHAMBER

THROAT (DAMPER LOCATION)

SMOKE SHELF

X ←4″→ Y P

BREAST

SLOPE OF FIREBACK

LINTEL

N O

ARCH

PLUMB LINE

E →

FIREBACK

UNDER FIRE

M K

doors rushes down the chimney's back side (*See arrows in Diagram A*), you must arrange somehow that it quickly gets mixed with the hot air going up the front side and then you have a constant circulation, around and around—and this you can get with a smoke-shelf.

CONSTRUCTION OF SMOKE-SHELF

Look at *Diagram A*. About twelve inches above the lower edge of the lintel or arch (*at Point Y*), on the back wall of the chimney or throat, there must be constructed a small shelf, called the smoke-shelf. This brick shelf, projecting from the back of the smoke chamber wall, out toward the front, is about three to four inches deep from *P* to *Y*. It is laid horizontally, completely across the base of the smoke chamber. This is the air-mixer, the function of which can easily be seen by the arrows in *Diagram A*, showing movement of air.

This is one of the most important features of Rumford's principles. This three-to four-inch deep opening is standard and must not vary, no matter how big the fireplace.

The cold air descends down the back wall of the chimney and hits this smoke-shelf. Since moving air must go somewhere, this cold current bounces off the shelf toward the front where it readily mixes with the hot air rising from the fire. This mixture then rises up the inside wall of the lintel. This action creates a continuous draft as the arrows demonstrate. I remember so well when I was a small boy living in northern Vermont, my cousin, Cecil Doten, a native mechanical genius of the old school, demonstrated this in a very practical fashion. He built and placed in this space a small wood-paddle windwheel. The constantly circulating air in the chimney kept it going. We thought that he had invented the wonder of the age, perpetual motion. He hadn't!

It is obviously essential, however, to maintain this perpetual circulation of cold air down and warm air up the chimney. The reason is that from the burning fire, three times more vapour, smoke and hot gasses will be generated and want to go up than the amount of radiant heat that ought to go out into the room. We must put nothing in the way of this vertical action. If we do, something will go out into the room that is never wanted:—I refer to smoke.

This is the significant reason for the smoke-shelf dimensions that Count Rumford so carefully worked out. Do not be discouraged if, sometimes, when you start a fire in a cold fireplace, you may get a little smoke before there is enough heat to start this proper circulation because it is circulation that does the job.

How most efficiently to project the radiant heat is the next problem. This is accomplished by proper relation of the angles, depth, height, and slant of sides and back. Rumford developed all these relationships as has been stated in order to cast the rays of heat out into the room.

The best fireplace, contrary to modern masons, is not deep and squatty, but shallow and high, with slanted sides and back!

{44}

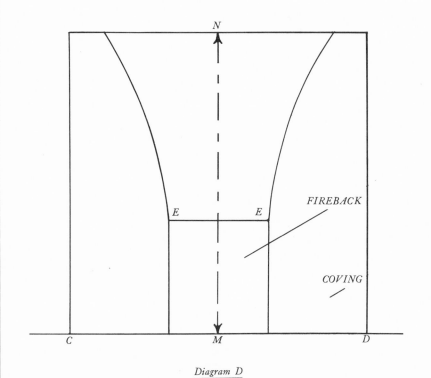

Diagram D

FRONT ELEVATION
SHOWING CURVED BACK WALL

PRACTICAL APPLICATION OF THE PRINCIPLES

Like all other geometric truths, as Rumford demonstrated, the dimensions or shape of the fireplace, no matter what size one is building, must always follow the same rules and have the same relationships to one another.

Let us look at *Diagram B, Plan View.*

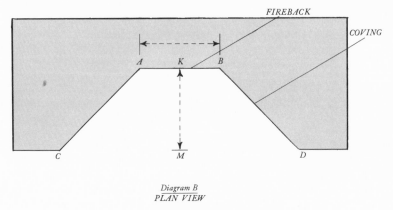

Diagram B
PLAN VIEW

OPENING C-D, THREE TIMES THE DEPTH M-K

The back wall of the fireplace opening (that is called the "Fire-Back", dimension A to B) should be the same as the depth (M to K).

Thus, if you plan to build a back wall fifteen inches wide (A to B), then you must arrange for a depth of fifteen inches (M to K). Remember all measurements in this diagram are on the floor of the hearth.

{46}

Next comes the important front opening. This dimension (C to D) can be *three times* the depth. With a
fifteen-inch depth, you will come up with a forty-five-
inch-wide opening (C to D). (*Diagram B*).

If these dimensions are followed, then the side walls or
covings of the fireplace, as Rumford called them, will
assume the correct slant or angle. (Covings are C to
A and D to B).

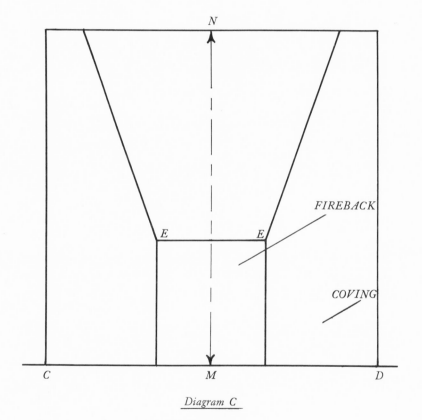

Diagram C

FRONT ELEVATION
SHOWING C-D AND M-N THREE TIMES THE DEPTH, MK

I have measured many fireplaces, including five in my own house. Some follow Count Rumford's principles of dimension perfectly and some very slightly. But one in my living room varies in respect to the front opening and the angles of the covings; and yet functions perfectly, as I have related. The enjoyable fireplace pictured as the frontispiece of this book has an opening 42 inches high and 42 inches wide. It is 19 inches deep and the back is 24 inches wide. This means that the sides slant, from the front, at an angle of only 65°.

Measurements I have taken of many other early American fireplaces in New England bear out my contention that if, for aesthetic reasons, one wishes to vary the angle of the covings, one may do so and not lessen the proper function of a fireplace.[3]

In other words, one may construct a fireplace front opening (C to D) that is less than *three* times the depth. It may be two times the depth, creating an angle from the front of 70°. I believe, however, that if I were building a new fireplace, I would stay within the area of from *two* to *three* times the depth, for aesthetic reasons. (See *Diagram B-2*).

Now, how about the most important feature, aesthetically, of your fireplace? This is the height of the front opening from hearth to the bottom of the lintel.

---

[3]*After all, the angle of the covings was established by Rumford most efficiently to throw the radiant heat into the room and warm the bodies in the room. If one is building a fireplace to obtain the most heat, the slant of the covings shown on page 46 (Diagram B) is preferable, but otherwise, for aesthetic reasons, a variation of this angle is permissible (shown Diagram B-2 opposite).*

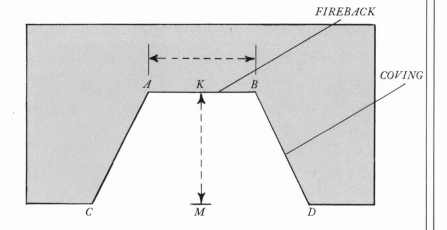

Diagram B-2
PLAN VIEW

OPENING C-D, *TWICE THE DEPTH M-K*

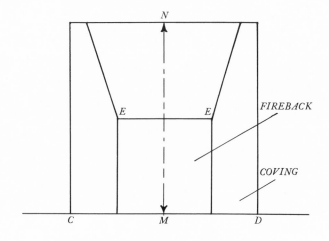

Diagram C2

FRONT ELEVATION
SHOWING C-D AND M-N TWICE THE DEPTH, MK

This is an interesting feature because the taller this opening the more pleasure one will obtain from the fireplace, watching the flames leap higher.

This opening may be as high as *three times* the depth! Thus, in *Diagram A*, the dimension of M to N, is three times the dimension of M to K. Still assuming we are building a fifteen-inch-deep fireplace, this will support a forty-five-inch-tall opening.

Here the reader may be startled. This is certainly a major departure from the low, deep box that modern masons delight in building and calling "fireplace". I have talked with many of them, and still don't know why they do it. I sometimes think they are under the impression they are building a box stove instead of a fireplace.

Here I must mention another modern abomination that I constantly see illustrated in some of the current "home" magazines. These, apparently, are made up by artists and writers who never left Madison Avenue. It is the squatty, deep fireplace, built so low that one can barely see the flame. But the talented artists and writers have remedied this defect by raising if *off the floor* on a brick hearth, a foot or more above the floor level! Not only do I consider this a monstrosity, but Count Rumford would turn over in his grave if he could see it. It is not only an aesthetic violation but it is completely unnecessary if one follows Count Rumford's designs. One can see and enjoy the fire in tall shallow fireplaces by leaving the hearth on the floor where it belongs.

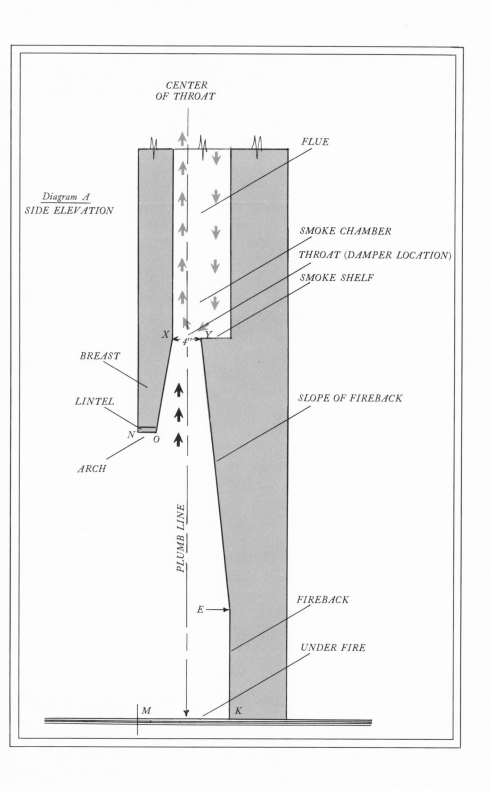

CENTER
OF THROAT

FLUE

Diagram A
SIDE ELEVATION

SMOKE CHAMBER

THROAT (DAMPER LOCATION)

SMOKE SHELF

X 4" Y

BREAST

SLOPE OF FIREBACK

LINTEL

N O

ARCH

PLUMB LINE

E

FIREBACK

UNDER FIRE

M K

THE SLOPE AT THE BACK OF THE FIREPLACE

Since Count Rumford advised that one must do everything possible to facilitate the vapours, smoke and gasses rising up the chimney instead of going into the room, one of his innovations was the determination of the proper forward slant of the back firewall.

See *Diagram A*. This area, K (at the base) to Y, should begin to slant forward at a point at E, or about fifteen inches above the hearth floor. It should then slant in an angle so that, about twelve inches above the lintel or arch, it forms on the back wall (at Y) the front of the smokeshelf.

See *Diagrams E and D* for another cross section and front elevation showing how this slanted back of the fireplace may be a curve, instead of a straight slant. The curved back is better looking than the straight but more difficult to build.

In revising, or reconstructing hundreds of old fireplaces in England, during his sojourn there, Count Rumford found that many of them, which had been smoking for years, could be corrected by adding this slant to the back wall. It was not necessary to tear down the whole thing and begin over. The same remedy may be applied to fireplaces today.

Another essential dimension may be corrected by rebuilding. This is the depth of the throat. See *Diagram A*, dimension X to Y. As emphasized before, this dimension should never be more than four inches or less than three. If this aperture is too big then the necessary

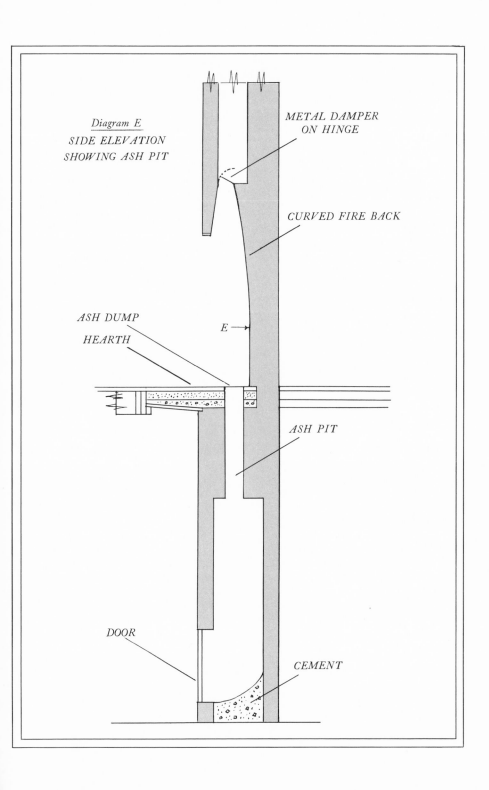

Diagram E
SIDE ELEVATION
SHOWING ASH PIT

METAL DAMPER
ON HINGE

CURVED FIRE BACK

ASH DUMP

HEARTH

E →

ASH PIT

DOOR

CEMENT

circulation is destroyed; cold air coming down will not mix with the warm air that wants to go up.

I again call attention to this fact, as I have looked at countless fireplaces built by modern masons and even some built years ago by ignorant masons only to find to my horror that this opening is several times four inches! And also to find, to my further sorrow, that often there is no smoke-shelf at all. The owners of such poor, weak fireplaces, complaining, as they must, that the fireplace smokes, are often advised by ignorant persons to build a copper or metal lip down the front to lower the lintel opening. That, they are told, will do it! It surely will. It will fill the room more quickly with more smoke and often put out the fire.

The Damper in the Fireplace

Since we are looking at this four-inch opening in the throat of the fireplace, I may as well indicate that this is the place for a damper if, when the fireplace is *not* in use, you want to prevent heat in the room from going up the chimney or cold air from coming down into the room (*See Diagram E*).

It is good to note that Benjamin Franklin also thought about this problem and, in his letter to Dr. Ingen-Hausz, speculated at length on its solution. He was worried about smoke that issued from chimneys of neighbors and in passing, as it was bound to, over the top of one's own chimney, got drawn down into the room during the daytime. To remedy this offense Franklin did not mention the word "damper" but came very near it by suggesting a "sliding plate" that would shut off completely the "offending funnel". *Rumford, however, developed the damper as we know it today.*

Franklin was a very charming character. Many of his notions come to us over the centuries laden with the same sweet charm as when his fertile mind and heart conceived them.

For example, he comments on the fact that there were many lecturers in "experimental philosophy" (an expression embracing all natural science then). He wishes they would give attention to experiments as part of their lectures. And here he describes one of his most delightful conceits: build a little model room, he says, composed of panes of glass, framed in wood at the corners, "with proportionable doors, and moveable glass chimneys, with openings of different sizes, and different lengths of funnel (as he called the chimneys), and some of the rooms so contrived as to communicate on occasion with others, so as to form different combinations and exemplify different cases; with quantities of green wax taper cut into pieces of an inch and a half, sixteen of which stuck together in a square, and lit, would make a strong fire for a little glass chimney, and blown out would continue to give smoke as long as desired. With such an apparatus, all the operations of smoke and rarified air in the rooms and chimneys might be seen through their transparent sides."

I would love to see such a charming little model constructed and, with instructions for experiments, given to each architect and mason in the land who proposes to design or build a fireplace . . . along, of course, with Count Rumford's principles.

But back to dampers in the chimney.

There are stock control dampers of cast iron or sheet metal so constructed that they will not destroy the function of the smoke-shelf or the important function of the four-inch-wide aperture. They are little doors on hinges that may be closed or opened by a hook or lever. If properly made and installed, they will lie flat on the smoke-shelf in back, flush to the inside wall of the lintel in front. If so installed, they will not interfere with the function of the smoke-shelf as an air mixer, when you do use the fireplace.

You will be surprised that, if all else is built right, you will be able to lay a fire on the front of the hearth that seems actually out in the room, yet the fire will burn, the flames leap up, and never a wisp of smoke enters the room. Never should you build it too big and raging. The inside of the chimney must be warm to make for perfect combustion, and this should be accomplished with deliberation and care.

That's all there is to it!

Helpful Aids

There are, however, other helpful aids in the proper construction of your fireplace. One is the proper size of the smoke chamber, that section above the smoke-shelf inside the fireplace. (*See Diagram F.*) This must be as wide at its base as the width of fireplace, C to D in *Diagram* C, and should slope upwards inside the chimney until it comes to a center in the middle of the flue. The inside area of a flue should be one-tenth of the area of the fireplace front opening. Thus, a fireplace forty inches high and thirty-nine inches wide, totaling 1560 square inches, should have a flue area of at least 156 square inches.[4]

---

[4]*Square flues are better and more efficient than round ones. Manufactured ceramic flues come in standard sizes from 8" x 12" to 24" x 24". It is recommended that one plan the fireplace based on size of flues available.*

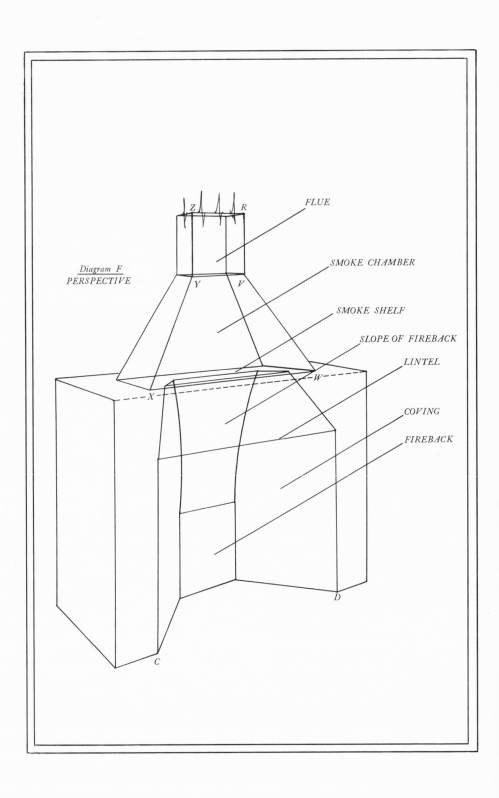

FLUE

SMOKE CHAMBER

SMOKE SHELF

SLOPE OF FIREBACK

LINTEL

COVING

FIREBACK

Diagram F
PERSPECTIVE

Since the best fire is one laid well forward on the hearth, it is important that the front inside walls, back of the lintel, be smooth, just as the inside of the water pipe is smooth. (*Diagram* A, dimension O to X). This helps the gases and smoke to ascend. Also, the total thickness of this front wall above the lintel (or arch) should be no more than five inches (N to O).

Rumford, and the few others who followed his basic ideas, cautioned against locating the fireplace near a window. The light from the window would lessen the pleasures of watching the charming glow of the fire and distract attention from the architectural beauty of the mantel, which would be especially true were one to be fortunate enough to have a carved mantel in the McIntire manner.

Rumford's book is full of wise and often witty observations, all practical—such as the one that a fireplace does not "draw" up heat and smoke. Heat and smoke rise by themselves, if given a chance.

Don't, he says, treat a fireplace as a refuse burner, or, I say, for getting rid of gobs of cloth, old tires, and garbage. Give the fire a chance for its life by burning good dry hard wood and make what Rumford constantly refers to as a "good, cheerful, clean, bright fire . . . not a sloven one." Clean fires burn less fuel.

Don't expect a fireplace to work well if you construct it of projecting jagged fieldstone or badly laid jagged brick. The inside of the fireplace and its chimney should be *smooth*. It should be made of brick, soapstone, or marble—not iron which absorbs heat. If you insist on building a fieldstone fireplace, better line it with smoothly laid brick or have the stone dressed. As a matter of fact, rough fieldstone fireplaces have no place in a home. They may be all right in a rural retreat or a log hunting lodge but not in a formal house.

Many even more obvious features are forgotten to-day, such as being sure the top of the chimney is at least three feet above the roof ridge, dormer windows, nearby trees, or surrounding buildings. Covings should extend to the jamb, not stop way behind it.

If you live at a place where high winds bother and try to force themselves down the chimney, that's easily corrected by building a pyramid or cone roof (chimney pot) over the chimney top.

One admonition that the good Count expressed would seldom obtain today. He cautioned against allowing women to march back and forth quickly in front of the fireplace, close to it. The clothes of the female would, he states, be apt to cause eddies in the air by which puffs of smoke might easily be brought into the room. I doubt if in our day women wear enough clothes to cause eddies of air. They may cause eddies — but not those that affect a fireplace.

NOTE FROM THE AUTHOR

Many readers have requested special advice regarding their unique problems or a discussion of their desire to change the Rumford specifications in the book for building proper fireplaces. I am informed by my attorneys that I am not a qualified architect and cannot legally establish an advisory service and dispense it. Therefore, I cannot enter into correspondence about this book. There are, however, two small matters on which I am glad to advise here:

1. BRICK OVENS. Brick ovens, the true name for ovens built next to the fireplaces, are not mentioned in this book because another book in THE FORGOTTEN ARTS series covers them specifically. For details on *The Forgotten Art of Building and Using a Brick Bake Oven*, see the back cover of this book.

2. DAMPERS. Fireplace dampers are usually manufactured of heavy cast iron and may be obtained from building contractors or plumbers who have sources of supply. Since these dampers are made by people who know nothing about how to build a proper fireplace, usually the opening is too wide. Naturally, the trap door opening in the damper, through which the smoke ascends from the fire, must never be wider than four inches. Also, I have seen some of these commercial dampers, and the frame which holds the trap door opening is usually so wide and heavy that care must be taken in installation. You cannot install such a damper with the heavy frame sticking out from the inside front surface of the smoke chamber opposite the smoke shelf. If you did so, it would obstruct the cir-

culation of the air. The disadvantages of such commercial dampers may be overcome if the mason is instructed to bury the front frame of the damper in the brick wall so that when installed, the inside (See the diagram below, Section O to X) is still relatively smooth. Another caution:- when the damper is installed, it must be adjusted so when the trap door is open, it will be perpendicular at the front edge of the smoke shelf. It is too bad that someone does not make a damper with a narrow frame, which can be installed flat on the smoke shelf and the trap door pulled forward when you want the opening of the fireplace closed. It would look something like this:

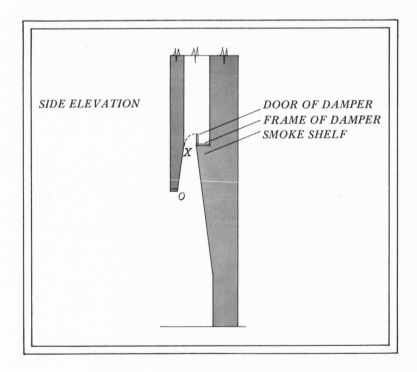

SIDE ELEVATION

DOOR OF DAMPER
FRAME OF DAMPER
SMOKE SHELF

X

O

COLOPHON

This Book was designed by Vrest Orton and set in Caslon, Monotype, ⚹337-E, a machine fount, designed as near as possible to conform with the original punches cut by William Caslon in England, about the year 1720. Caslon Old-style has been widely used by all great printers from 18th century Benjamin Franklin, to 20th century Bruce Rogers, Carl Purrington Rollins, Daniel Berkeley Updike and other great American typographers whose work in the 1920s has never been equalled or surpassed in the United States.

ABOUT THE AUTHOR

VREST ORTON, who was born in Vermont, left the state at an early age. He served in World War I in France and, after leaving Harvard in the early 1920s, he was briefly with the U.S. Consular Service in Mexico, going to New York City in 1925 to join the staff of H.L. Mencken's *American Mercury* (and later *The Saturday Review)*. In 1929, he founded the international book collectors' magazine *The Colophon.*

Returning to Vermont from the Pentagon after World War II, Mr. Orton and his wife, Ellen, founded the nationally known Vermont Country Store and its mail-order catalog, *The Voice of the Mountains.*

Active in state affairs for many years, Mr. Orton was elected a delegate to two national Republican Conventions and for ten years served as Chairman of *The Vermont Historic Sites Commission* and as Vice President of *The Vermont Historical Society.* In 1946, he was a founder and for some years an editor of *Vermont Life* magazine. In the mid-50s he was elected President of the *American Association of Historic Sites Public Officials* and in 1958 was appointed by President Eisenhower to serve on the federal commission commemorating the 350th anniversary of the discovery of Lake Champlain. He also served as a consultant to The Department of Defense, Washington, D.C.; and to the Ford Motor Company, Dearborn, Michigan.

In addition to operating the Vermont Country Stores with his son Lyman, Vrest Orton writes articles for national magazines and newspapers. Since 1970, he has had published four books: — *Calvin Coolidge's Unique Vermont Inauguration, Vermont Afternoons with Robert Frost, The Homemade Beer Book,* and *The American Cider Book.*

Vrest Orton is married, has three sons, Geoffrey, Lyman and Jeremy, and lives in an old brick house with five fireplaces on the Village Green in Weston, Vermont.